Ferdinand Magellan

Jane Gould

PowerKiDS
press

New York

Published in 2013 by The Rosen Publishing Group, Inc.

29 East 21st Street, New York, NY 10010

First Edition

Editor: Joanne Randolph

Book Design: Planman Technologies

Illustrations: Planman Technologies

Library of Congress Cataloging-in-Publication Data

Gould, Jane H.

Ferdinand Magellan / by Jane Gould. — 1st ed.

    p. cm. — (Jr. graphic famous explorers)

Includes index.

ISBN 978-1-4777-0069-3 (library binding) — ISBN 978-1-4777-0123-2 (pbk.) — ISBN 978-1-4777-0124-9 (6-pack)

1. Magalhães, Fernão de, d. 1521—Travel—Juvenile literature.
2. Explorers—Portugal—Biography—Juvenile literature.
3. Voyages around the world—Juvenile literature. I. Title.

G286.M2G64 2013

910.92—dc23

[B]

                                2012018694

Manufactured in the United States of America

CPSIA Compliance Information: Batch #W13PK1: For Further Information contact Rosen Publishing, New York, New York at 1-800-237-9932

Contents

Introduction

Ferdinand Magellan led the very first **expedition** to sail around the world. He left Spain in September 1519 with five ships and a crew of about 250 men. Three years later, one ship made it back to Spain with just 18 men aboard. Magellan was not one of them. Before he died, though, he found a pathway between the Atlantic Ocean and the Pacific Ocean, now called the **Strait** of Magellan. Today people remember Magellan for his remarkable achievement and for proving that it is possible to sail all the way around the world.

Main Characters

Ferdinand Magellan (1480–1521) Leader of the expedition that was the first to sail around the world.

King Charles I of Spain (1500–1558) Spanish ruler who supported Magellan's voyage. Charles was named king of Spain in 1516 and Holy Roman Emperor Charles V in 1519.

Diego Barbosa (c. 1500s) Magellan's father-in-law, who helped him get the backing he needed for his voyage. Barbosa was an **influential** man in Seville, and he had ties to the rich and influential men in Spain.

Humabon (c. 1500s) The ruler of the Pacific island of Cebu who wanted Magellan's help to defeat his enemy. Following his conversion to Christianity, he took the name Carlos.

Juan Sebastián de Elcano (c. 1476–1526) The last **commander** of Magellan's **fleet**, who completed the journey around the world. Elcano started the expedition as master of the *Concepción*.

FERDINAND MAGELLAN

UNTIL MAGELLAN'S VOYAGE, PEOPLE'S IDEA OF HOW THE WORLD LOOKED WAS VERY DIFFERENT FROM TODAY'S.

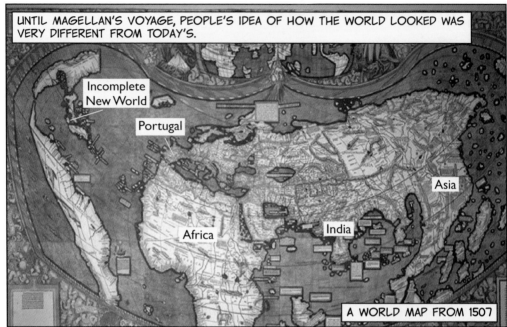

A WORLD MAP FROM 1507

MAGELLAN WAS BORN IN PORTUGAL IN 1480. WHEN HE WAS 12, HE BECAME A **PAGE** TO THE QUEEN OF PORTUGAL. AT COURT, HE LEARNED MATH, NAVIGATION, AND ASTRONOMY.

EUROPEANS WERE TRYING TO FIND SEA ROUTES TO ASIA. PORTUGUESE EXPLORERS WERE THE FIRST TO SAIL AROUND AFRICA'S CAPE OF GOOD HOPE TO INDIA. PORTUGAL CLAIMED CONTROL OF THAT WHOLE AREA.

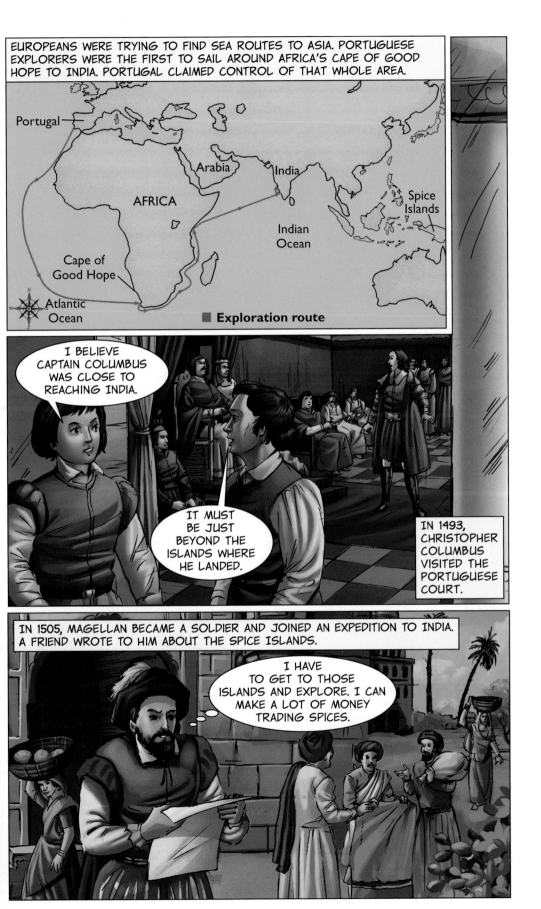

I BELIEVE CAPTAIN COLUMBUS WAS CLOSE TO REACHING INDIA.

IT MUST BE JUST BEYOND THE ISLANDS WHERE HE LANDED.

IN 1493, CHRISTOPHER COLUMBUS VISITED THE PORTUGUESE COURT.

IN 1505, MAGELLAN BECAME A SOLDIER AND JOINED AN EXPEDITION TO INDIA. A FRIEND WROTE TO HIM ABOUT THE SPICE ISLANDS.

I HAVE TO GET TO THOSE ISLANDS AND EXPLORE. I CAN MAKE A LOT OF MONEY TRADING SPICES.

It took a while for Magellan to achieve his dream. While fighting in India and North Africa, he was wounded three times.

When he was 34, Magellan went back to Portugal.

MAGELLAN WENT TO THE KING OF PORTUGAL AND DESCRIBED HIS PLAN TO SAIL TO THE SPICE ISLANDS. MAGELLAN NEEDED MONEY FOR SHIPS AND SUPPLIES.

YOUR MAJESTY, I AM SURE THAT THIS IS A SHORTER ROUTE THAN THE ONE AROUND AFRICA.

WHY SHOULD I HELP YOU? THE ROUTE WE HAVE HAS PROVED ITSELF SUCCESSFUL. YOU HAVE NOT.

THE SPANISH HAVE NOT FOUND RICHES IN THE LANDS THEY CONTROL. THEY HAVE TO GO TO ASIA TO FIND **CLOVES** AND NUTMEG.

IMAGINE WHAT SPAIN WOULD DO TO HAVE ITS OWN SPICE TRADE!

SOUTH AMERICA CURVES LIKE AFRICA. THERE ARE RUMORS THAT YOU CAN SAIL AROUND OR THROUGH THE BOTTOM.

NO ONE HAS FOUND A PASSAGE YET.

I WILL.

NO ONE KNEW IF THERE WAS A WESTWARD SEA ROUTE TO ASIA. MAGELLAN STUDIED MAPS AND TALKED TO PEOPLE WHO HAD BEEN TO SOUTH AMERICA.

7

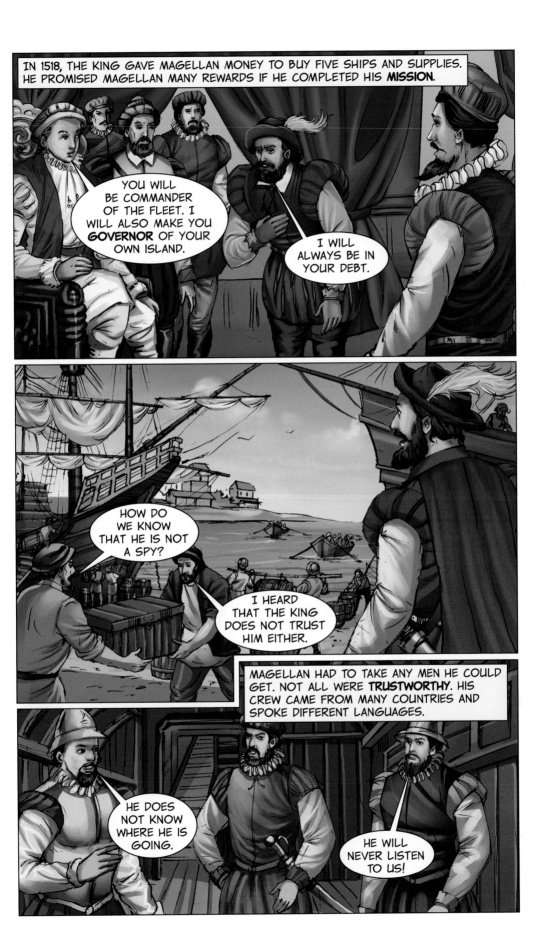

WHEN THEY WERE FINALLY READY TO SET SAIL, MAGELLAN COMMANDED THE BEST OF THE SHIPS, THE *TRINIDAD*. THE OTHER FOUR SHIPS HAD THEIR OWN CAPTAINS.

YOUR SHIPS WILL ALWAYS FOLLOW MINE. YOU MUST OBEY ALL MY ORDERS.

SOON AFTER LEAVING PORT, BAD WEATHER SET IN. ONE OF MAGELLAN'S CAPTAINS WOULD NOT OBEY ORDERS. HE TRIED TO **MUTINY**. MAGELLAN LOCKED HIM UP IN ANOTHER SHIP.

I AM NOT THE ONLY ONE WHO DOES NOT TRUST YOU.

YOU WILL BE LOCKED UP UNTIL YOU OBEY ME. THE CREW WILL SEE WHO IS IN COMMAND!

MAGELLAN HAD TO BE CAREFUL TO STAY AWAY FROM PORTUGAL'S **TERRITORY**. PORTUGAL WAS ANGRY THAT SPAIN WANTED TO TAKE OVER THE SPICE TRADE.

WE NEED TO BE CAREFUL NEAR THE AFRICAN COAST.

PORTUGAL WILL HAVE SHIPS WAITING TO ATTACK US.

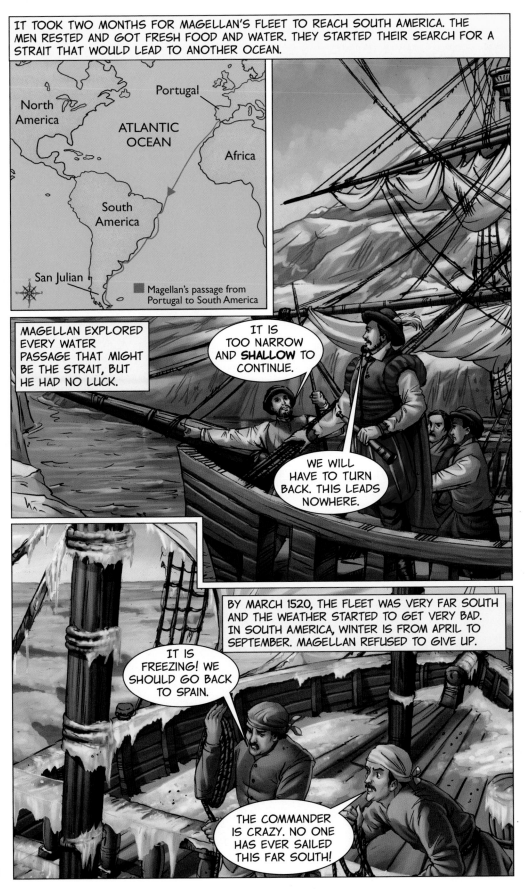

IT TOOK TWO MONTHS FOR MAGELLAN'S FLEET TO REACH SOUTH AMERICA. THE MEN RESTED AND GOT FRESH FOOD AND WATER. THEY STARTED THEIR SEARCH FOR A STRAIT THAT WOULD LEAD TO ANOTHER OCEAN.

North America

Portugal

ATLANTIC OCEAN

Africa

South America

San Julian

Magellan's passage from Portugal to South America

MAGELLAN EXPLORED EVERY WATER PASSAGE THAT MIGHT BE THE STRAIT, BUT HE HAD NO LUCK.

IT IS TOO NARROW AND **SHALLOW** TO CONTINUE.

WE WILL HAVE TO TURN BACK. THIS LEADS NOWHERE.

BY MARCH 1520, THE FLEET WAS VERY FAR SOUTH AND THE WEATHER STARTED TO GET VERY BAD. IN SOUTH AMERICA, WINTER IS FROM APRIL TO SEPTEMBER. MAGELLAN REFUSED TO GIVE UP.

IT IS FREEZING! WE SHOULD GO BACK TO SPAIN.

THE COMMANDER IS CRAZY. NO ONE HAS EVER SAILED THIS FAR SOUTH!

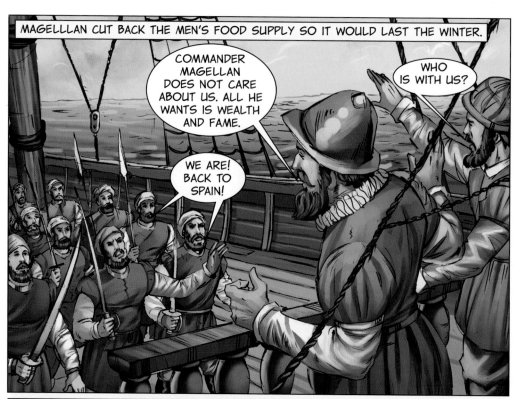

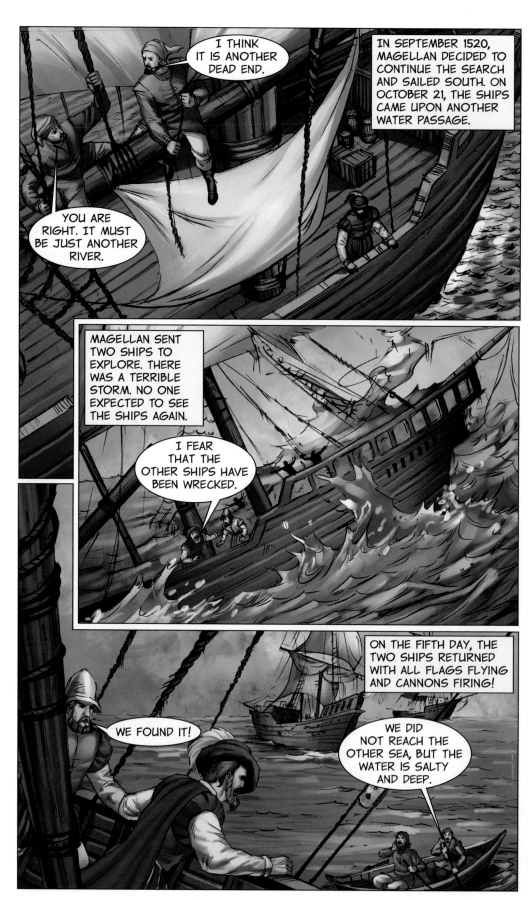

IT WAS NOT EASY FOR THEM TO FIND THEIR WAY THROUGH THE NARROW STRAIT. THERE WERE MANY **INLETS** TO EXPLORE.

SOUTH AMERICA

Atlantic Ocean

Inútil Bay

Canal Whiteside

Tierra del Fuego

Pacific Ocean

■ Route through the Magellan Strait

HIGH WINDS AND STRONG **CURRENTS** THREATENED TO SMASH THE SHIPS.

STEER CLEAR! WATCH FOR THOSE ROCKS!

FINALLY, THE MEN SAW THE FIRES OF **NATIVE** PEOPLE IN THE DISTANCE. THE SPANIARDS CALLED THE AREA *TIERRA DEL FUEGO*, OR LAND OF FIRE.

THERE MUST BE MANY PEOPLE LIVING THERE.

MAGELLAN HAD NO IDEA HOW BIG THE PACIFIC OCEAN WAS. THE SHIPS SAILED FOR MONTHS. THE MEN WERE FORCED TO EAT RATS AND LEATHER. MANY GOT SICK AND DIED.

TWICE MAGELLAN TRIED TO LAND ON ISLANDS. ONE ISLAND HAD LITTLE FOOD OR WATER. THE OTHER HAD NATIVE PEOPLE WHO WERE NOT FRIENDLY.

MEN SUFFERED FROM **SCURVY** AND THE TERRIBLE HEAT. IN MARCH 1521, AFTER ALMOST FOUR MONTHS, THE SHIPS REACHED AN ISLAND WITH FRIENDLY NATIVES, FOOD, AND FRESH WATER.

MAGELLAN SAILED TO NEARBY ISLANDS, KNOWN TODAY AS THE PHILIPPINES.

THE LANGUAGE SPOKEN HERE IS LIKE THE LANGUAGE OF THE SPICE ISLANDS.

THE SPICES THEY GAVE US PROVE THAT WE ARE NEAR.

MAGELLAN LANDED ON AN ISLAND CALLED CEBU. HE MADE FRIENDS WITH THE RULER, NAMED HUMABON. HUMABON AGREED TO MAKE CEBU PART OF SPAIN. HE ALSO AGREED THAT HIS PEOPLE WOULD BECOME CHRISTIAN.

WE MUST BE POLITE TO OUR GUEST. I WILL DO AS HE ASKS WHILE HE IS HERE.

THE KING ADMIRES YOUR WEAPONS. HELP HIM DEFEAT LAPU LAPU AND CLAIM MACTAN FOR SPAIN.

HUMABON TOLD MAGELLAN THAT THE ISLAND OF MACTAN WOULD NOT BECOME CHRISTIAN OR OBEY THE SPANISH. LAPU LAPU, THE RULER OF MACTAN, WAS HUMABON'S ENEMY.

MAGELLAN WENT TO MACTAN, BURNED VILLAGES, AND DEMANDED SUPPLIES. ON APRIL 27, 1521, MAGELLAN AND 60 ARMED MEN RETURNED TO THE ISLAND.

SIR, THERE IS A CORAL REEF. WE CANNOT TAKE THE BOATS ANY FARTHER.

AS THE MEN REACHED THE SHORE, THEY WERE SOON SURROUNDED BY HUNDREDS OF NATIVES WITH BOWS AND SPEARS. MAGELLAN WAS ATTACKED AND KILLED.

SAVE YOURSELVES!

HUMABON WAS ANGRY THAT THE SPANIARDS HAD LOST. AFTER HE KILLED A FEW OF THE CREW, THE REST OF THE MEN ESCAPED AND QUICKLY SAILED AWAY.

I WISH WE DID NOT HAVE TO BURN THAT THIRD SHIP.

WE HAVE BARELY ENOUGH MEN TO SAIL TWO SHIPS.

THE LAST TWO SHIPS HEADED FOR THE SPICE ISLANDS. AFTER ALMOST SIX MONTHS, THEY FINALLY REACHED THEM. WHILE THERE, THEY LOADED THE SHIPS WITH CLOVES, CINNAMON, AND OTHER VALUABLE SPICES.

WE HAVE TO TAKE BACK AS MUCH AS THE SHIPS CAN CARRY.

ONE SHIP HAD A LEAK AND COULD NOT LEAVE. THE LAST SHIP, THE *VICTORIA*, SAILED WITH JUST 50 MEN ABOARD. THE SHIP'S NEW CAPTAIN WAS JUAN SEBASTIÁN DE ELCANO.

WE WILL CONTINUE WEST.

IT IS A PROTECTED PORTUGUESE ROUTE. WE WILL HAVE TO BE CAREFUL.

THE *VICTORIA* ROUNDED THE CAPE OF GOOD HOPE AND FINALLY ARRIVED IN SPAIN ON SEPTEMBER 6, 1522. THE CREW WAS THE FIRST TO CIRCLE THE GLOBE. THE 18 SURVIVING MEN WERE EXHAUSTED AND SICK, BUT THEY RECEIVED A JOYFUL WELCOME.

I THOUGHT I WOULD NEVER SEE MY HOME AGAIN.

WE HAVE BEEN GONE ALMOST EXACTLY THREE YEARS!

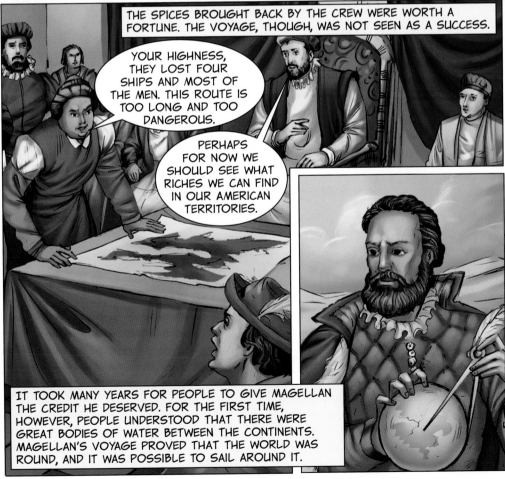

THE SPICES BROUGHT BACK BY THE CREW WERE WORTH A FORTUNE. THE VOYAGE, THOUGH, WAS NOT SEEN AS A SUCCESS.

YOUR HIGHNESS, THEY LOST FOUR SHIPS AND MOST OF THE MEN. THIS ROUTE IS TOO LONG AND TOO DANGEROUS.

PERHAPS FOR NOW WE SHOULD SEE WHAT RICHES WE CAN FIND IN OUR AMERICAN TERRITORIES.

IT TOOK MANY YEARS FOR PEOPLE TO GIVE MAGELLAN THE CREDIT HE DESERVED. FOR THE FIRST TIME, HOWEVER, PEOPLE UNDERSTOOD THAT THERE WERE GREAT BODIES OF WATER BETWEEN THE CONTINENTS. MAGELLAN'S VOYAGE PROVED THAT THE WORLD WAS ROUND, AND IT WAS POSSIBLE TO SAIL AROUND IT.

Timeline and Map

1480   Magellan is born.

1493   Magellan goes to the court of the king of Portugal to serve as a page.

1505   Magellan joins an expedition to India and starts his military service.

1513   Magellan returns to Portugal and resumes his studies.

1517   Magellan marries Beatriz Barbosa, the daughter of a wealthy Portuguese merchant. His father-in-law helps Magellan get an introduction to the king of Spain.

1518   Magellan moves to Spain. In March, King Charles I agrees to sponsor Magellan's voyage to the Spice Islands.

1519   In September, Magellan begins his voyage. He reaches South America in November.

1520   On October 21, Magellan discovers a strait. It takes 38 days to sail through the strait to reach the Pacific Ocean.

1521   In March, Magellan reaches the islands now known as the Philippines. He is killed on the island of Mactan on April 27. The rest of his men continue to the Spice Islands, where they arrive in November.

1522   Juan Sebastián de Elcano sails the remaining ship back to Spain. It arrives in September, completing the first journey around the world. There are only 18 survivors.

Map of Magellan's Route

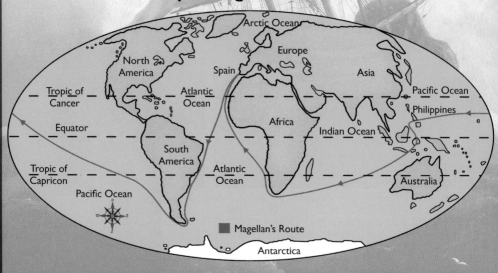

Glossary

bleak (BLEEK) Barren, depressing, gloomy.

cloves (KLOHVZ) A kind of valuable spice that grows in tropical climates.

commander (kuh-MAN-dur) The person in charge of a ship or of a military force.

currents (KUR-ents) Water that flows in one direction.

deserted (dih-ZUR-tid) To have left a place illegally, without permission.

expedition (ek-spuh-DIH-shun) A trip for a special purpose.

fleet (FLEET) Many ships under the command of one person.

governor (GUH-vun-ur) An official who is put in charge by a king or queen.

influential (in-floo-ENT-shul) Having the power to sway others.

inlets (IN-lets) Narrow waterways.

mission (MIH-shun) A special job.

mutiny (MYOO-tuh-nee) To disobey a captain's orders or revolt against a commanding officer.

native (NAY-tiv) Born or grown in a certain place or country.

page (PAYJ) A boy who works as an assistant to a knight or a young man who works at the royal court.

scurvy (SKUR-vee) A disease resulting from a deficiency of vitamin C, characterized by weakness and bleeding from mucous membranes.

shallow (SHA-loh) Not deep.

strait (STRAYT) A narrow waterway connecting two larger bodies of water.

territory (TER-uh-tor-ee) Land that is controlled by a person or a group of people.

trustworthy (TRUST-wur-thee) Dependable and honest.

Index

Websites

Due to the changing nature of Internet links, PowerKids Press has developed an online list of Websites related to the subject of this book. This site is updated regularly. Please use this link to access the list:

www.powerkidslinks.com/jgff/mage/